The author, Veda Wilhite, at the age of nine dressed for her school play.

Fabric Requirements:

All projects in this book are scrap quilts. You will need several fat quarters or half yard cuts of Red, Blue, Brown, Tan, Gold and Black fabrics.

A Special Thanks to

Karen O'Neill, owner of the Cabbage Rose Quilting and Gifts shop, for all her help and encouragement.

My sister, Janice Smith, for editing.

My nephew, Mark Smith, for all his help with my computer and for enlarging my world.

My husband, Sonny, for his support and gracious acceptance of numerous sandwich meals.

My family and friends for their wonderful support and encouragement.

This book is dedicated to the men and women who gave their all for freedom's cause when they were called.

Patterns are used with permission from Veda Wilhite, America: The Pride of My Heart, originally © 1998 - Veda Wilhite and May We Never Forget, originally © 2001 - Veda Wilhite.

Table of Contents

America...
the Pride of My Heart Quilt

If you have ever taken a "Block of the Month" class. you know how much fun it is to make a large quilt a little at a time. Some of these blocks are very simple patches. Others give you the opportunity to practice your piecing and appliqué skills. If your group is looking for a quilt project to raffle off as a fundraiser. you should definitely consider this one.

Patriotic quilts have a wide appeal to the general public and this quilt can be made quickly when each person makes one or two blocks.

see instructions on pages 22 - 45

Large Eagle Pillow

This eagle bears an olive branch, an international symbol of the peace we all pray for. This pillow is just one example of how you can take the patterns from this quilt and use them to create home decor projects. I love appliqué because it is portable and I can sit with my family and friends while I work on it.

For those who love unique table runners, this star block combination is just for you. I hope you enjoy making these patterns for every room in your home.

Many of us have loved ones serving our country overseas. It is so important to let our servicemen and women know how much we appreciate their sacrifice so we may all live in peace and comfort. Nothing lifts their spirits and improves morale like receiving a special gift from home. I remember the "care packages" we sent during WWII. They were packed with love, personal items and treats.

Today, security concerns and the strain on the mail system prohibit sending packages, but we can still participate in the lives of our loved ones with e-mail and the "Gifts from the Home Front" gift certificate program. These certificates can be sent to a particular serviceman or sent to someone you don't even know. Go to www.aafes.com or 1-877-770-4438 for more information to help you remember the special someone on their birthday with an expression of your gratitude and care.

"Operation Dear Abby" allows you to send a Sailor, Marine, Soldier, Airman, or Coast Guardsman a greeting or message of support. Servicemen and women with internet access read the messages via "OperationDearAbby.net". For those without internet access, company commanders print and distribute the messages.

Please do not underestimate the importance or impact of sending a simple e-mail. You can make a difference in the lives of Americans doing a difficult task and living in difficult conditions. For more information on sending your support, go to www.anyservicemember.navy.mil.

see instructions on pages 64 - 65

Quilt Block Pillows
Colorful Pillows for Every Room in Your Home

If you love flags as much as I do, you will want to make a flag pillow first. The star block can be as simple as a starry print or any pieced star design you like. Put a border around the edge and your pillow is almost done.

see basic pillow assembly instructions on page 63

Santa

Merry Christmas, America! Take some time to enjoy quilting for your loved ones during this season of peace. As I quilt this wonderful block, I pray for all of our servicemen and women working overseas. They have given up being with their loved ones so that we can all enjoy a safe holiday season. I give thanks for each and every one of them.

see instructions on pages 41 - 43

Large Flag

I love flags. Every time I see one, my heart fills with pride and gratitude for all this great nation has provided. This large flag makes the perfect "Welcome" wall hanging for your front porch.

see instructions on pages 28 - 30

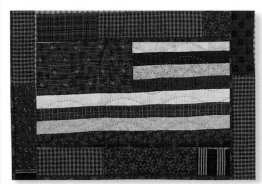

Small Flag

For those with limited space for displaying wall hangings, this small flag will meet your needs. Express your love of country with this quick to make project. This also makes a great pincushion.

see instructions on page 31

Remember... Flag Wall Hanging

I think every American remembers where they were and what they were doing on September 11, 2001, just as the previous generation knows exactly where they were on December 7, 1941. In just a few hours time, we all moved from disbelief to shock to tears to anger to an overwhelming desire to help and support each other. My expression of that support is this Flag. It was so important to make something from my heart. Every stitch represents a constant prayer for the victims of this tragedy and their families and friends, as well as for all our public officials who had the responsibility of leading us out of the chaos and finding ways to deal with the aftermath.

see instructions on pages 46 - 49

On Eagle's Wings Quilt

The girls who work at the Cabbage Rose Quilting and Gifts shop in Fort Worth, Texas made this quilt for Shea O'Neill, who was beginning a new career as a firefighter after working with his mom, Karen, for a couple of years in the shop. During this time, he so graciously put up with all us women with a smile on his face. As a token of appreciation, we presented him with this quilt.

Shea,
You never know how high you can fly until you try.
So, aim for the sky and soar on eagle's wings
And don't ever forget how special you are.

"On Eagle's Wings" was designed and pieced by Veda Wilhite, machine quilted by Connie Thurston. The large eagle block was quilted by Veda Wilhite in 2002.

This quilt is dedicated to America's real heroes who paid the ultimate price on Sept. 11, 2001. Fire, police, and military men and women, and average citizens from all walks of life who gave their all...in lower Manhattan in the World Trade Center...at the nation's capital in the Pentagon...in the air above and on the grassy field in Pennsylvania. "May we never forget."

Let your American spirit soar with this high-flying "On Eagle's Wings" quilt. As I worked on this quilt, the words from the beloved song. "Wind Beneath My Wings". by Bette Midler were constantly on my mind.

"Did you ever know that you're my hero. and everything I would like to be?
I can fly higher than an eagle. for you are the wind beneath my wings."

see instructions on pages 50 - 61

Stars Table Runner

Patriotism is the love of, devotion to, and willingness to serve one's country. My gratitude for the freedoms I enjoy is the source of my deep sense of patriotism. I express my love of country with quilts and other home decor that I designed. Use individual blocks or combinations of blocks to make wall hangings and table runners. The small star blocks will add a bit of red, white, and blue to the bottom of a towel for the kitchen or bath. These small blocks also make lovely book covers.

see instructions on page 62

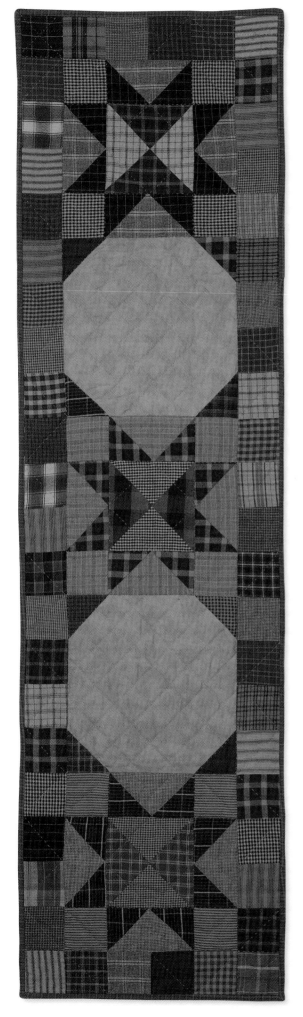

Quilt Block Pillows
Pillows for Every Sofa

Patriotic pillows bring a bit of red, white and blue to any decor. Any block in this quilt can be made into a pillow. Toss a couple on the couch, or in your favorite chair. Decorate the kitchen chair with the All American Basket. Make some star pillows for the guest bedroom. Before you know it, you will have a house full of these pretty projects.

see basic pillow assembly instructions on page 63

Ohio Star

Make this star in rich earth tones. Then scatter this masculine design for chairs in your den or library. Don't forget these make nice chair backs too!

star on page 22

Victory Basket

Turn this basket pattern into a place mat and napkin set. Put it in your picnic basket now and it will be ready for the 4th of July family outing.

basket on pages 26 - 27

8 Point Star

My great technique allows you to piece this wonderful star without sewing on the bias. You are really going to enjoy making this block.

star on page 25

America... the Pride of My Heart Quilt
pages 22 - 45

Large Ohio Star
page 22

Small Ohio Star
page 23

Friendship Star
page 24

Eight Point Star
page 25

Victory Basket
pages 26 - 27

Sawtooth Star
pages 28 - 29

Large Flag
page 30

Small Flag
page 31

Tiny Flag
page 36

Churn Dash
page 32

Nine Patch
page 32

Appliqué Star
page 33

Pieced Star
pages 38 - 39

Santa Block
pages 41 - 43

Directory
of Patterns and Instructions

"On Eagle's Wings" Quilt
pages 53 - 61

Prairie Star
pages 50 - 51

Alternate Block
page 52

Medium Eagle
pages 34 - 37

Flag Wall Hanging
pages 46 - 48

Stars Table Runner
page 62

Large Appliqué Eagle Pillow
pages 53 - 59, 64

Red Eagle Pillow
page 66

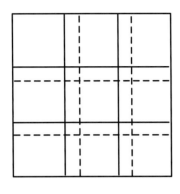

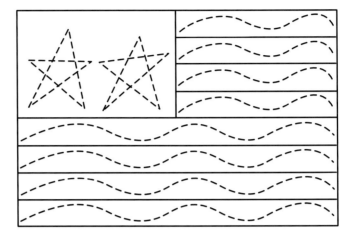

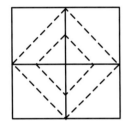

I used the same quilting design in all nine-patch and four square blocks.

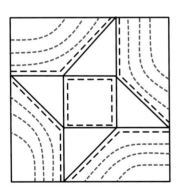

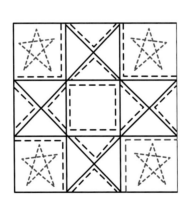

I used a lot of echo and in-the-ditch quilting.

I quilted in the ditch around every block.

Utility quilting = ----------

Regular quilting = ----------

Tips for Quilters

Suggestions for Quilting on Your Blocks

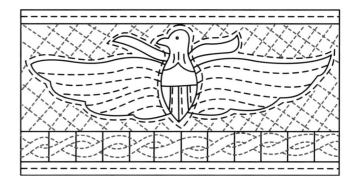

For the borders. I quilted in the ditch on the first narrow border. On the wider border. I utility quilted straight across the edge of the scrap border about 1 1/4" apart.

These are a few examples of quilting designs to help get you started. Do whatever you want and have fun with it.

Happy Quilting.

Veda

On the quilt labels:

ON EAGLE'S WINGS
Designed and pieced by Veda Kilhite
Machine quilted by Connie Thurston
Eagle block quilted by Veda Kilhite   2002

This quilt is dedicated to America's real heroes who paid the ultimate price on Sept. 11, 2001. Fire, police, and military men and women and average citizens from all walks of life gave their all... in lower Manhattan in the World Trade Centre... at the nation's capital in the Pentagon... in the air above and on a grassy field in _____... May we never forget.

AMERICA the Pride of My Heart
Pieced in 1998 as a Block of the Month for the Cabbage Rose, Fort Worth, Texas. Made its debut at the Houston International Quilt Festival in Nov. 1998. Completed quilting in May 2000.
Veda Kilhite   Fort Worth, Texas

Label Your Quilts

I cannot stress enough how important it is that you label your quilts. Your quilt is a work of art as valid as any museum masterpiece.

Sign it, date it, and if possible, give some clues as to why you made it! This label is a perfect example.

Quilts make a wonderful gift for that special someone in your life.

When you put your label on the back, be sure to include words to let them know what they have meant to you. All too often, we leave things unsaid that need to be said.

General Instructions

Please read all instructions before beginning.

SEAMS:

All rotary cutting instructions include $^1/_4$" seam allowance. It is very important that your seams are an exact quarter of an inch.

Check your pressure foot on your sewing machine using a piece of layout bond grid paper (4 squares per inch). With the edge of your pressure foot on one line, your needle should come down directly on the next line.

I love piecing quilts like this because every block is different. Piecing the blocks together is like working a jigsaw puzzle. I get the same thrill when the pieced blocks fit and interlock together.

THREAD:

Use 100% cotton thread for piecing. When I appliqué, I prefer using Gutermann 100% silk thread. This thread is hard to find sometimes. If you can't find it, Mettler cotton thread for machine embroidery also works well. Both are great for hand appliqué.

I hand-quilted this quilt using regular hand quilting and utility quilting. For the regular hand quilting, I used YLI Quilting Thread (Light Brown #3) and for utility quilting I used DMC Cotton Perlé #8 (color #640).

FABRIC:

100% cotton fabric is recommended. I advise you to wash all fabrics. Some fabrics do bleed and should be washed until the rinse water is clear.

Even though you are using all 100% cotton fabrics, some may shrink more than others, giving a puckered seam.

Pre-washed fabric is much easier to hand-quilt and hand-appliqué because of all the sizing and excess dye has been washed out.

Also, pre-washed fabric bonds together better, thus making it easier to machine-piece.

I wash my fabric by hand with a few drops of very mild detergent, rinse, spin dry in the washing machine, dry in the dryer, and press.

If I have a large piece of fabric, more than a yard, I will wash it in the washing machine on gentle. I really don't like to use the washing machine because the fabric will ravel badly.

WOOL FABRIC:

I often like to use 100% wool fabric that has been felted (by washing in hot water) for appliqué, such as on the eagle bodies and wings. It is wonderful to work with because the edges do not fray or need to be turned under.

Simply stitch around the edges using a Blanket Stitch for stitching by hand, or use a decorative stitch when stitching by machine.

continued on pages 20 - 21

APPLIQUÉ:

You may use your favorite method of appliqué. I love to hand-appliqué. It is so relaxing and it is something you can easily carry with you to work on in the car, the doctor's waiting room, or wherever. Of all the methods I have tried, I like this freezer paper method the best.

Trace the appliqué pattern on the paper side of the freezer paper. Cut the pattern out directly on the line and iron it on the right side of the fabric.

Draw a thin line along the edges of the freezer paper pattern with an ultra-fine point permanent marker. DO NOT mark any edges of the pattern that will be underneath another pattern piece, just leave a $1/4$" seam along these edges.

Cut the pattern out leaving a $1/8$" - $1/4$" seam all around. You will trim this seam as you appliqué. Be sure to leave the freezer paper on until after you have cut it out in order to hold the fabric stable.

Position pattern pieces and baste or glue in place. Roxanne Glue-Baste-It is great for this.

Remove the freezer paper, fold the edge in to the drawn line and secure with an appliqué stitch (sometimes called a blind stitch or slip-stitch). Using small stitches approximately $1/8$" apart, continue stitching all around the edge tucking in as you go with your needle or finger.

If you will be sure to barely catch the very edge of the fold line with your needle your stitches will be almost invisible.

BINDING THE EDGE OF A QUILT

A beautiful binding provides the same finishing touch for your quilt that a proper frame gives a Rembrandt painting. You have invested a lot of time, money, love, and care into this masterpiece.

Follow the steps below to give your work its finishing touch.

Then, remember to sign your work with a proper label (see the beautiful samples on page 18).

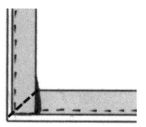

1. I start in the corner and go along the first side with a $1/4$" seam, stopping $1/4$" from the edge.

Then I stitch a slant to the corner (through both layers of binding)... lift up, then down, lining up the edge.

2. Then I continue stitching the next side with a $1/4$" seam.

3. When I come to the starting corner, I miter this one corner. This way I don't have any bulk on any side.

4. Fold over to the back and pin. Tuck under the edge and hand-stitch to secure.

PERFECT TWO-TRIANGLE SQUARES:

I don't like to work with triangles or work on the bias. Therefore, throughout this project, I will be showing you different methods that I use to avoid triangles.

For the perfect two-triangle square, layer two fabric squares right sides together.

Draw a diagonal line from corner to corner on the wrong side of the Lighter fabric.

Sew $1/4$" from each side of the diagonal line.

Cut on the diagonal line and press open toward the Dark.

This makes 2 two-triangle squares.

Using your square mini-rule, square up these two-triangle squares to the size you need.

Line up the diagonal line of the square with diagonal line on mini-rule and trim a little bit on two to four sides to make a perfect two-triangle square.

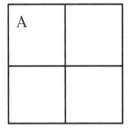

FILLER BLOCKS:

There are 56 four-inch finished blocks in this quilt. I used four different styles. Three of these are shown at right. I used thirty-eight A squares, seven B squares, and seven C squares.

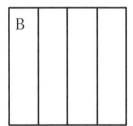

A. Four $2^1/2$" squares
B. Four $1^1/2$" x $4^1/2$" strips
C. Two $2^1/2$" x $4^1/2$" strips

The fourth filler block is the Flying Geese.

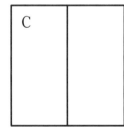

FLYING GEESE

Cut one Light $2^1/2$" x $4^1/2$" rectangle and two Dark $2^1/2$" squares. Layer one $2^1/2$" square on right side of rectangle. Stitch from corner to corner (Diagram 1). Trim away middle section of corner. DO NOT CUT BACK. USE THIS TO LINE UP BLOCK. Press open and repeat with $2^1/2$" square on left side of rectangle (Diagram 2). Trim middle section and press open (Diagram 3). If your corners do line up perfectly when you press them up, you may cut away both sections instead of only the middle section as I told you before. This will make it easier to hand-quilt.

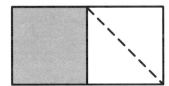
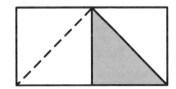
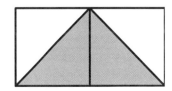

My thanks to Mary Ellen Hopkins for this connector square method.

Large Ohio Star
from America... the Pride of My Heart Quilt

photo on pages 4 - 5

Month 1
This Quilt Makes a Great 'Block of the Month' project

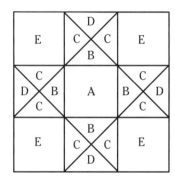

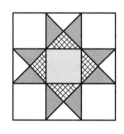

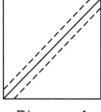 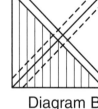 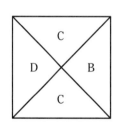

Diagram A   Diagram B   Diagram C

Freedom is a blessing that every American holds dear to their heart. The willingness to fight for freedom is what makes America great.

LARGE OHIO STAR - $12^1/_2$" (12" finished)

Rotary cut

A = One $4^1/_2$" sq. (Navy print)
B = One $5^1/_2$" sq. (Gold Plaid)
C = Two $5^1/_2$" sqs. (Light Blue Plaid)
D = One $5^1/_2$" sq. (Light print)
E = Four $4^1/_2$" squares (Light print)

Place one C square and the B square right sides together. On wrong side of Lighter fabric draw a diagonal line corner to corner. Stitch $1/_4$" from drawn line on both sides (Diagram A). Cut on drawn line.

You now have 2 two-triangle squares. Press seam toward Darker fabric. Repeat with the other C square and the D square. With right sides of contrasting triangles facing, place C and B triangle square atop C and D triangle square.

Center diagonal seam of each interlocking seam. Draw a diagonal line from opposite corner to corner. Stitch $1/_4$" from line on both sides (Diagram B). Cut on drawn line.

Repeat with remaining C-B and C-D triangle squares. You now have 4 four-triangle units (Diagram C).

Trim each four-triangle square to $4^1/_2$" lining up diagonal line as you do for the perfect two-triangle square.

The difference is that you need to use a little math and center on the diagonal line.

Example: for a $4^1/_2$" square (cutting size), center at $2^1/_4$" and then trim to $4^1/_2$".

Sew units together as shown.

This should be a $12^1/_2$" square (12" finished).

Small Ohio Stars
from America... the Pride of My Heart Quilt
photo on pages 4 - 5

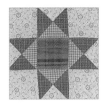

I am always amazed by the generosity Americans have. American quilters have always been first to respond with busy needles when there is a critical need. If you haven't made a charity quilt lately. use up your scraps by making a collection of 8" stars and sew them into a quilt for your favorite charity.

SMALL OHIO STARS - 8$^1/_2$" (8" finished)

BLOCK A - RED

Rotary cut

    A = One 3" square (Red Plaid)
    B = One 4" square (Tiny Red Check)
    C = Two 4" squares (Brown Plaid)
    D = One 4" square (Light print)
    E = Four 3" squares (Light print)

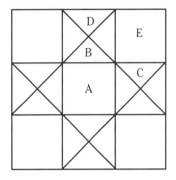
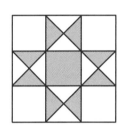

Use same piecing method as in 12" finished Ohio Star.

Trim each four-triangle square to 3". This makes an 8" (7$^1/_2$" finished) block.

Piece one 1" x 8" strip (Red Plaid) to top of block.

Piece one 1" x 8$^1/_2$" strip (Dark Brown Plaid) to left side of block.

You now have a 8$^1/_2$" (8" finished) block.

BLOCK B - BLUE

Rotary cut

Use the same cutting sizes as shown above with only two fabrics.

    A and C = Navy Plaid
    B, D, and E = Light print

Use same piecing method as in 12" finished Ohio Star.

Trim each four-triangle square to 3". This makes an 8" (7$^1/_2$" finished) block.

Piece one 1" x 8" strip (Navy print) to bottom of block.

Piece one 1" x 8$^1/_2$" strip (Brown print) to right side of block.

You now have a 8$^1/_2$" (8" finished) block.

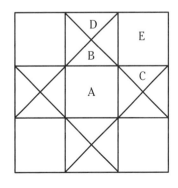
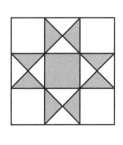

Friendship Star
from America... the Pride of My Heart Quilt
photo on pages 4 - 5

The bonds formed between men fighting for freedom often last forever. Celebrate those special friendships with this Friendship Star block.

Month 2
This Quilt Makes a Great 'Block of the Month' project

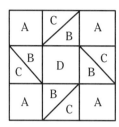

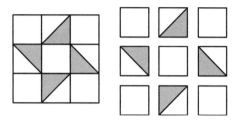

LARGE FRIENDSHIP STAR - $8^1/2$" (8" finished)

Rotary cut
 A = Four 3" sqs. (Red Stripe)
 B = Two $3^1/2$" sqs. (Red Plaid)
 C = Two $3^1/2$" sqs. (Light print)
 D = One 3" sq. (Gold print)

Using perfect two-triangle method, join two C squares to the two B squares. You now have 4 two-triangle squares. Trim each two-triangle square to 3".
 Join all units together as shown.
 You now have an 8" ($7^1/2$" finished) block.
 Cut a 1" x 8" strip of Brown print and piece to top of block.
 Cut a 1" x $8^1/2$" strip of Red and piece to right side of block.

You now have an $8^1/2$" (8" finished) block.

SMALL FRIENDSHIP STAR - $6^1/2$" (6" finished)

Rotary cut
 A = Four $2^1/2$" sqs. (Light print)
 B = Two 3" sqs. (Blue Plaid)
 C = Two 3" sqs. (Light print)
 D = One $2^1/2$" sq. (Red Stripe)

Use the same directions as above.
Trim each two-triangle square to $2^1/2$".
You do not need to strip this block.

The soldier on the left is Joe Bennett. one of my ancestors who fought for freedom during World War I.

Eight Point Star
from America... the Pride of My Heart Quilt

photo on pages 4 - 5

It's easy to avoid sewing parallelograms for this Eight Point Star when you use the "Perfect Two-Triangle Square" technique. This complicated-looking star, also known as the "Eastern Star", becomes a simple 16-square patch.

There are three different sizes of this block used in the quilt. All three are pieced the same way.

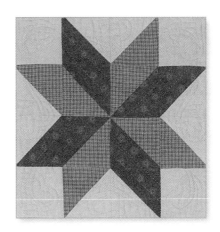

EIGHT-POINT STAR
For each star join:
    2 B sqs. to 2 C sqs.
    2 B sqs. to 2 D sqs.
    2 C sqs. to 2 D sqs.

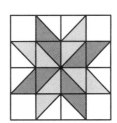

Trim each two-triangle square to size shown below and join each unit together as shown.

LARGE EIGHT-POINT STAR - 16" finished
Rotary cut
    A = Four $4^1/_2$" sqs. (Light print)
    B = Four 5" sqs. (Light print)
    C = Four 5" sqs. (Navy print)
    D = Four 5" sqs. (Blue Plaid)
Trim two-triangle sqs. to $4^1/_2$".
Block should be $16^1/_2$" sq. (16" finished)

MEDIUM EIGHT-POINT STAR - 8" finished
Rotary cut
    A = Four $2^1/_2$" sqs. (Light print)
    B = Four 3" sqs. (Light print)
    C = Four 3" sqs. (Blue Plaid)
    D = Four 3" sqs. (Gold print)

Trim two-triangle sqs. to $2^1/_2$".
Block should be $8^1/_2$" sq. (8" finished)

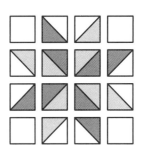

SMALL EIGHT-POINT STAR - 6" finished
Rotary cut
    A = Four 2" sqs. (Light print)
    B = Four $2^1/_2$" sqs. (Light print)
    C = Four $2^1/_2$" sqs. (Red Plaid)
    D = Four $2^1/_2$" sqs. (Red Check)

Trim two-triangle sqs. to 2" sqs.
Block should be $6^1/_2$" sq. (6" finished)

Month 3
This Quilt Makes a Great 'Block of the Month' project

Victory Basket
from America... the Pride of My Heart Quilt
photo on pages 4 - 5

Month 4
**This Quilt Makes a Great
'Block of the Month' project**

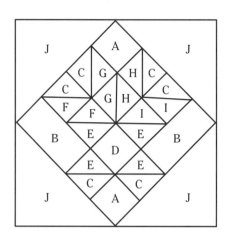

One of my childhood memories is of the Victory gardens during World War II. Almost everyone had a garden in their yard to provide food for their families and friends. These were called Victory Gardens.

Some items were rationed during the war years because they were so scarce. I remember that sugar, coffee, shoes, tires, silk hose and gasoline were some of the items rationed. Sometimes they were so scarce that even if you had the money and the ration stamps, you still could not get them. I thought it was wonderful when people shared their ration stamps with those in need.

When I was around eight years old, I attended a Masonic Temple Shriner's picnic at Eagle Mountain Lake with my family. I could not swim and almost drowned when I fell off the dock. There were several people at this picnic, but only one man saw me go under. He jumped in, clothes, watch, shoes and all. His name was Bill Baird of Mrs. Baird's Bakery and I owe him my life.

My father told him there was no way he could ever repay him, but he had one thing he could give him. He gave him his shoe ration stamp. Bill Baird gladly accepted this token of gratitude, for even though he had the money, he couldn't buy a new pair of shoes without the stamp and he had ruined his when he jumped into the water to save me.

As for my own token of gratitude, to this day I still buy Mrs. Baird's Bread here in Texas.

14$^1/_2$" block, 14" finished

Rotary cut:

Background (Tan print)
    A = Two 3" sqs.
    B = Two 3" x 5$^1/_2$" rectangles
    C = Five 3$^1/_2$" sqs.
Basket (Navy print)
    D = One 3" sq.
    E = Three 3$^1/_2$" sqs.
Petal #1 (Red Check)
    F = Two 3$^1/_2$" sqs.
Petal #2 (Light Blue print)
    G = Two 3$^1/_2$" sqs.
Petal #3 (Red print)
    H = Two 3$^1/_2$" sqs.
Petal #4 (Brown Plaid)
    I = Two 3$^1/_2$" sqs.

Triangle Border (Red Plaid)
    J = Two 8" sqs.
    Cut these in half diagonally.

Diagram 1

Delicious Brownies

Enjoy this All-American Basket with another All-American favorite - chocolate brownies! This basket would make a lovely place mat on your luncheon table.

Using the perfect two-triangle method, join together the following squares:
C-E, C-F, C-G, C-H, C-I, F-E, G-H, I-E

Trim these two triangle squares to 3". You will have an extra square of each of these except for C-E.

Sew units together as shown in Diagram 1.
Sew a triangle J to each side of the block.
Square up the block to $14^1/2$" (14" finished).

- 1 cup Crisco Oil
- 2 cups sugar
- 2 teaspoons vanilla
- 4 eggs
- 1 cup flour
- $^2/_3$ cup dry cocoa
- $^1/_2$ teaspoon baking powder
- $^1/_2$ teaspoon salt
- chopped nuts

Mix all ingredients together and bake in a greased and floured 10" x 15" pan at 350 degrees for 25 minutes.

Icing

Heat together:

- 4 tablespoons dry cocoa
- $^1/_2$ stick margarine
- 5-6 tablespoons milk

Add powdered sugar and beat until icing is of spreading consistency. Spread over brownies while still warm.

Sawtooth Star Within a Star
from America... the Pride of My Heart Quilt

photo on pages 4 - 5

Month 5

This Quilt Makes a Great 'Block of the Month' project

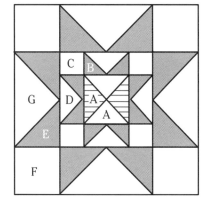

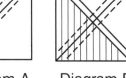

Diagram A   Diagram B

When you really like a block design and don't know why, it is time to examine the design elements in that block so you can apply them to other projects.

This "Sawtooth Star Within a Star" uses repetition and symmetry. The traditional Sawtooth Star uses a solid block in the center.

Repeating the design in a smaller size adds interest to the block. You can also substitute any other block you like for the center to make your own unique designs.

$12^1/_2$" (12" finished)

Rotary cut

A - Center = 2 contrasting $4^1/_2$" sqs.
   (Red Stripe, Blue Plaid)
B - Points = Four $2^3/_8$" sqs. (Navy print)
C - Corners - Four 2" sqs. (Tan and Red print)
D - Geese - One $4^1/_4$" sq. (Tan and Red print)
E - Points - Four $3^7/_8$" sqs. (Red Plaid)
F - Corners - Four $3^1/_2$" sqs. (Tan and Red print)
G - Geese - One $7^1/_4$" sq. (Tan and Red print)

Place two contrasting $4^1/_2$" squares right sides together. On wrong side of Lighter fabric draw a diagonal line corner to corner. Stitch $1/_4$" from drawn line on both sides (Diagram A).

Cut on drawn line. You now have 2 two-triangle squares. Press seam toward Darker fabric. With right sides of contrasting triangles facing, place triangle square atop triangle square. Center diagonal seam of each interlocking seam.

Draw a diagonal line from opposite corner to corner. Stitch $1/_4$" from line on both sides (Diagram B).

Cut on drawn line.

You now have 2 four-triangle units. One unit = one center square. You will have an extra four-triangle unit.

Trim each four-triangle square to $3^1/_2$", lining up diagonal line as you do for the perfect two-triangle square.

Since this is to be trimmed to $3^1/_2$" square, you will center on the diagonal line at $1^3/_4$".

With right sides together, place 2 point squares (B) on opposite corners of "geese" square (D).

Draw a line diagonally from corner to corner and stitch $1/4$" from line on both sides (Diagram A). Cut along drawn line and press points up (Diagram B). Place remaining point squares on each "geese".

Draw a line diagonally from corner to corner and stitch $1/4$" from this line on both sides (Diagram C). Cut along drawn line and press points up.

You now have 4 sets of "geese" or star points. Sew units together as shown.

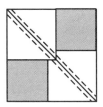 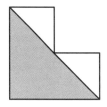 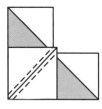

Diagram A   Diagram B   Diagram C

After you have completed this Sawtooth Star unit (A,B,C and D), you will have a $6^1/2$" sq. (6" finished), which you will use as the center of your 12" block.

This 12" star is put together the same way, using E,F,G, and the $6^1/2$" Sawtooth Star block.

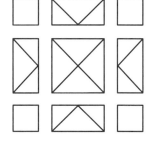

I learned this method at a retreat and I do not know the source. Since I didn't have my sewing machine. I didn't try to put one together until I got home. After many hours and repeated attempts. I finally figured the method out.

My thanks to whoever is responsible for this wonderful technique.

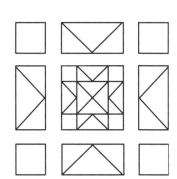

SMALL SAWTOOTH STAR - $6^1/2$" (6" finished)

Rotary cut

A - Center = $3^1/2$" sq. (Blue w/stars)
B - Points = Four $2^3/8$" sqs. (Gold print)
C - Corners = Four 2" sqs. (Light w/Blue Stripes)
D - Geese = $4^1/4$" sq. (Light w/Blue Stripes)

This block is put together using the same method as above.

The only difference is your center square is one square instead of a four-triangle square.

Large Flag
from America... the Pride of My Heart Quilt
photo on pages 4 - 5

There is so much that every American should never forget.

I recall so vividly where I was on December 7, 1941. I was in my grandmother's kitchen when the news came over the radio that the Japanese had bombed Pearl Harbor. I recall the shock, the disbelief, and the tears. Although I was too young to comprehend the full impact, I knew something terrible had happened. I also remember the call to war the men received.

Let us never forget the sacrifices made by so many for our security and freedom.

Month 6
This Quilt Makes a Great 'Block of the Month' project

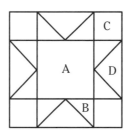

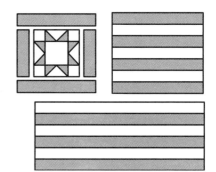

FLAG - 20^1/$_2$" x 24^1/$_2$" (20" x 24" Finished)

SAWTOOTH STAR - 8^1/$_2$" (8" finished)
Rotary Cut:
  A. Center = One 4^1/$_2$" sq. (Blue Plaid)
  B. Points = Four 2^7/$_8$" sqs. (Dark Blue print)
  C. Corners = Four 2^1/$_2$" sqs. (Light)
  D. Geese = One 5^1/$_4$" sq. (Light)
  Cut two strips 1^1/$_2$" x 8^1/$_2$" for sides (Navy print)
  Cut two strips 1^3/$_4$" x 10^1/$_2$" for top and bottom (Navy print)

Piece star block using instructions on Sawtooth Star on pages 28-29.
  Strip both sides with 1^1/$_2$" x 8^1/$_2$" strips, then strip the top and bottom with 1^3/$_4$" x10^1/$_2$" strips. This makes the block 10^1/$_2$" x 11" (10" x 10^1/$_2$" finished).
  These strips are four different Navy print fabrics.

FLAG STRIPES -
Rotary Cut:
  Red - Cut four 2" x 15"   Light - Cut three 2" x 15"
       Cut two 2" x 25"   Cut two 2" x 25"
       Cut one 2^1/$_4$" x 25"   Cut one 2^1/$_4$" x 25"
All Red and Light Stripes are different fabrics.
  Piece the four Red and three Light 2" x 15" Stripes together as shown. Trim these to 14^1/$_2$" and stitch to the right side of the Sawtooth Star block. Piece the 25" Red and Light Stripes together with the two wider Stripes on the bottom. Trim these to 24^1/$_2$" and stitch to the flag top.*
  I actually played with the six Stripes on the bottom, adjusting my seams to fit in the space 10" x 24^1/$_2$" (9^1/$_2$" x 24" finished). By making the two bottom Stripes a little wider, I'm making it easier for you.
  *When sewing several strips together, it is hard to keep perfectly straight on the sides. I usually cut my strips longer that the pattern calls for, then I trim sides to the correct size.

Small Flag
from America... the Pride of My Heart Quilt
photo on pages 4 - 5

I love the Fourth of July holiday when our nation's flag is displayed more than any other time. As I take in the beauty of the red, white and blue, I wonder why every month can't be like the month of July. I fly my flag every day, because every morning as I see the sun rise, I am thankful for the gift of another day in this wonderful country - the land of the free and the home of the brave.

These cutting instructions are for 1 flag. Remember that you need two flags for the quilt.

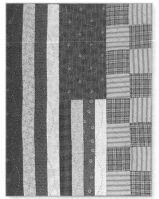

$8^1/_2$"x $16^1/_2$" (8"x 16" Finished)

Rotary Cut:
Blue Field - $4^1/_2$" x $8^1/_2$" (Blue with stars)
Red Stripes:
　Two $1^1/_2$" x 9"
　Two $1^1/_2$" x 17"
Light Stripes:
　Two $1^1/_2$" x 9"
　Two $1^1/_2$" x 17"

Month 7
This Quilt Makes a Great 'Block of the Month' project

All Red and Light Stripes are different fabrics.
Piece the Red and Light $1^1/_2$" x 9" strips together as shown.
Trim to $8^1/_2$" and piece to the right side of Blue field.
Piece the Red and Light $1^1/_2$" x 17" strips together as shown.
Trim to $16^1/_2$" and piece to bottom of first unit.

Cut eight $2^1/_2$" squares (Blue Stripe) and eight $2^1/_2$" squares (Red Plaid).
With these sixteen squares, piece four 4-patch squares (4" finished).
Piece these 4-patch squares together and sew to the top of one of the flag blocks.

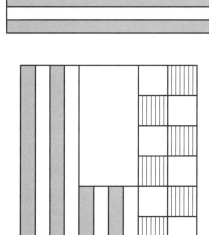

Churn Dash
from America... the Pride of My Heart Quilt
photo on pages 4 - 5

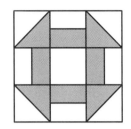

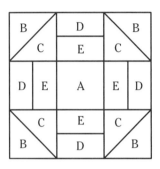

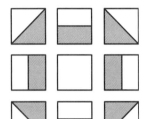

Month 8
This Quilt Makes a Great 'Block of the Month' project

I love old-fashioned traditional blocks. As I considered what blocks to put in the quilt, the Churn Dash block naturally came to mind. I didn't think it really fit the theme of the quilt until I attended a workshop by Terry Clothier Thompson who has designs and patterns in Barbara Brackman's book, "Quilts from the Civil War".

Terry talked about the Churn Dash block and said it was also known as "Sherman's March" and "Lincoln's Platform". I knew then that the Churn Dash block was a perfect choice for my patriotic quilt. If you haven't read Barbara's book, I recommend it. I found it very interesting and inspiring.

BROWN CHURN DASH BLOCK $6^{1}/_{2}$" (6" Finished)
Rotary Cut:
A = $2^{1}/_{2}$" sq. (Tan print)
B = Two 3" sqs. (Tan print)
C = Two 3" sqs. (Brown Plaid)
D = Four $1^{1}/_{2}$" x $2^{1}/_{2}$" rectangles (Tan print)
E = Four $1^{1}/_{2}$" x $2^{1}/_{2}$" rectangles (Brown Plaid)

NAVY CHURN DASH BLOCK $6^{1}/_{2}$" (6" Finished)
Rotary Cut:
A = One $2^{1}/_{2}$" sq. (Light Stripe)
B = Two 3" sqs. (Light Stripe)
C = Two 3" sqs. (Navy Plaid)
D = Four $1^{1}/_{2}$" x $2^{1}/_{2}$" rectangles (Light Stripe)
E = Four $1^{1}/_{2}$" x $2^{1}/_{2}$" rectangles (Navy Plaid)

Using the perfect two-triangle method, join each B square to each C square.

Trim each two-triangle square to $2^{1}/_{2}$". Join unit together as shown.

Nine Patch
from America... the Pride of My Heart Quilt

Diagram A   Diagram B

NINE PATCH - $6^{1}/_{2}$" (6" finished)

Rotary cut
Nine $2^{1}/_{2}$" squares

There are nine of these 9-patch blocks in this quilt. Seven of these have five Dark-medium squares and four Light-medium squares (A).

The other two blocks have five Light-medium squares and four Dark-medium squares (B).

Red, Blue and Brown fabrics are used in the nine-patch blocks.

Appliqué Star
from America... the Pride of My Heart Quilt

photo on pages 4 - 5

While you are in the mood to appliqué. this star is a quick and easy project. It is perfect for the beginner to learn appliqué. This block is a wonderful opportunity to share your patriotism and sewing skills with your grandchild.

Fill the afternoon with stories of relatives who have served their country. This is the best way to pass your values to the next generation.

Month 9
This Quilt Makes a Great 'Block of the Month' project

$8^1/_2$" (8" finished)

Rotary cut

Four 5" sqs. (Lights - All different)
Four 5" sqs. (Dark - Red Plaid, Brown print, Red Stripe, and Navy print)

Using perfect two-triangle method, join each Dark 5" sq. to each Light 5" sq.
Trim to $4^1/_2$" squares.
Join together as shown with all Light triangles in center.
You will have four extra two-triangle squares.
Appliqué a Gold Plaid star to the center.

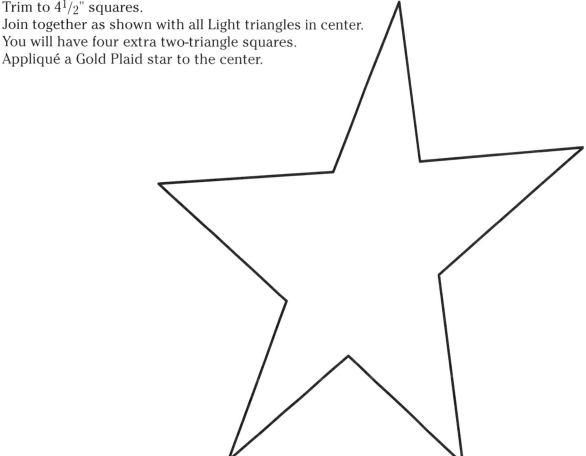

Medium Eagle on Quilt
from America... the Pride of My Heart Quilt
photo on pages 4 - 5

Month 9
continued
**This Quilt Makes a Great
'Block of the Month' project**

For six years the founding fathers of this nation debated the choice of a national symbol. They wanted an animal that was unique to the United States that symbolized strength and courage.

In 1782, they finally decided upon the bald eagle. The name "bald" derives from "piebald", meaning "marked with white". The Great Seal of the United States and Presidential flag both use the image of this treasured native bird.

Now you can appliqué your own great symbol of our national spirit.

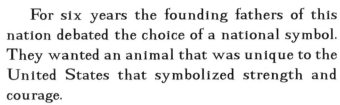

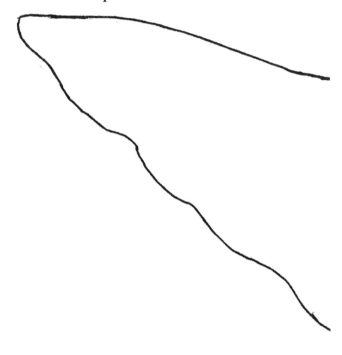

$12^1/_2$" x $24^1/_2$" (12" x 24" finished)

   Background - Navy print
   Wings - Gray Plaid (Wings are one piece)
   Shield - Red Stripe
   Top of shield- Navy with stars
   Banner - Tan
   Head - White
   Beak - Gold Plaid
Letters - *DMC* #898 embroidery floss = Outline stitch with 3 strands
Eye - Black embroidery floss = Colonial knot with 4 strands

   Cut background piece 9" x 25". After you have finished the appliqué and embroidery, trim to $8^1/_2$" x $24^1/_2$".
   Piece a row of twelve $2^1/_2$" squares to bottom of block.
   Piece a $1^1/_2$" x $24^1/_2$" strip of Red to top of block.
   Piece a $1^1/_2$" x $24^1/_2$" strip of Gold print to bottom of block.
This makes it $12^1/_2$" x $24^1/_2$" (12" x 24" finished).

Medium Eagle on Quilt
from America... the Pride of My Heart Quilt
photo on pages 4 - 5

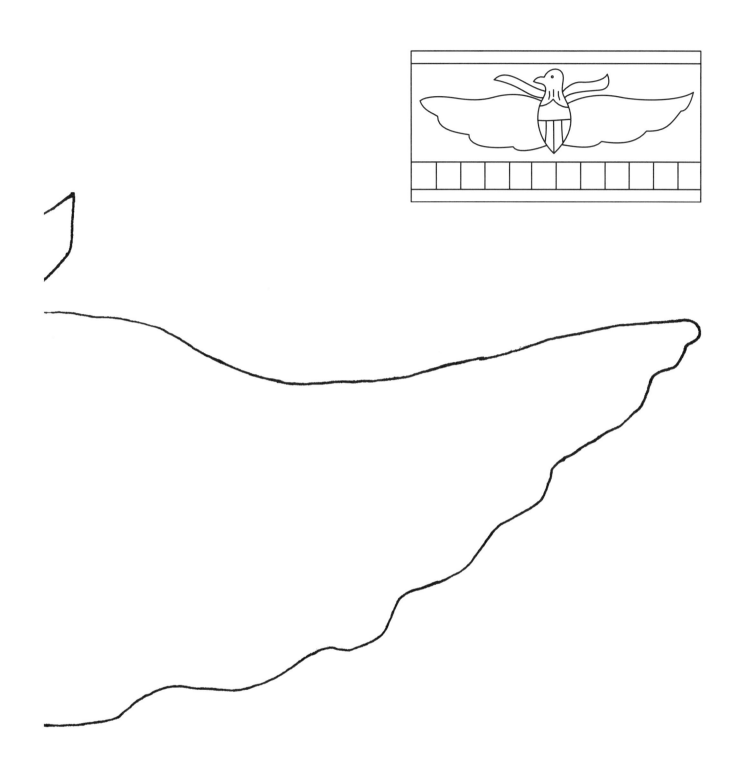

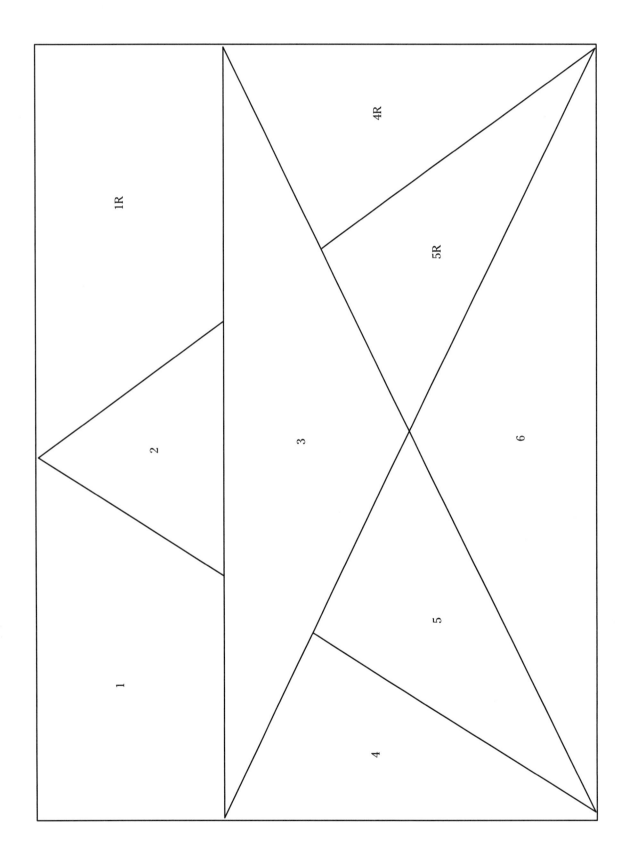

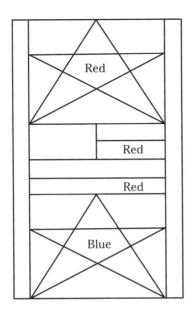

Star Blocks
from America... the Pride of My Heart Quilt
photo on pages 4 - 5

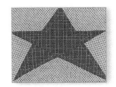

Month 10
**This Quilt Makes a Great
'Block of the Month' project**

These Star blocks are pieced together using freezer paper templates. I typically try to avoid templates if I can, but sometimes it is necessary. When I must use a template, I use freezer paper as the template material. I trace the pattern on the plain paper side of the freezer paper using the sewing line as the guide. Then, I cut the finished size template and iron to the wrong side of the fabric.

Using my acrylic ruler, I cut out the pattern piece with my rotary cutter leaving a $1/4$" seam allowance all around the edges. I don't draw cutting lines for templates because they are so easy to distort.

Sometimes I remove the freezer paper and sew as usual with a $1/4$" seam allowance. When I have a star pattern, I leave the paper on the fabric and use the edge of the paper as a guideline for sewing. Just pin each corner and center as you would do when you hand-piece, then sew along the edge of the freezer paper. Leave the freezer paper in place until you've sewn the entire block.

If you prefer to hand-piece these star blocks, please feel free to do so. This also works great.

STAR BLOCK:

Rotary cut
  $6^1/_2$" x $8^1/_2$" (6" x 8" finished)

BLUE STAR :
  1, 1r, 4, 4r, and 6 = Light print
  2, 3, 5, and 5r = Navy print

RED STAR:
  1, 1r, 4, 4r, and 6 = Light print
  2, 3, 5, and 5r = Red Plaid

Piece each star together in this order:
  5r and 4r - Unit A
  1, 2, and 1r - Unit B
  4, 5, and 6 - Unit C

Piece unit A to center template (3) then unit B and unit C.

One year after our marriage, my husband, Sonny, entered the United States Army. This picture was taken at Fort Hood, Texas in 1953.

Flag Block
from America... the Pride of My Heart Quilt
photo on pages 4 - 5

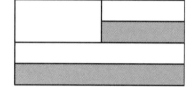

Whenever I see The Red. White and Blue waving in the wind. my heart fills with pride. The wonders of this great country and its people never cease to amaze me.

As I have watched the way the American people come together with love. comfort. and a helping hand after every devastating tragedy that befalls our nation. I am reminded once again of what makes this country great. The show of courage. determination. and steadfast faith shown by the victims is so touching. How can anyone not be affected by this?

As the words of the song say. "This is my country.....land that I love."

$4^1/_2$" x $8^1/_2$" (4" x 8" finished)

Rotary cut
　　One $2^1/_2$" x $4^1/_2$" = Blue
　　Two $1^1/_2$" x $4^1/_2$" = One Red and one Tan
　　Two $1^1/_2$" x $8^1/_2$" = One Red and one Tan
Piece together as shown.

Stars and Flag Block

$10^1/_2$" x $16^1/_2$" (10" x 16" finished)

Piece the flag and star blocks together as shown.
You now have an $8^1/_2$" x $16^1/_2$" (8" x 16" finished) block.
Cut a strip $1^1/_2$" x $16^1/_2$" (Red print) and piece to left side of block.
Cut a strip $1^1/_2$" x $16^1/_2$" (Navy print) and piece to right side of block.
You now have a $10^1/_2$" x $16^1/_2$" (10" x 16" finished) block.

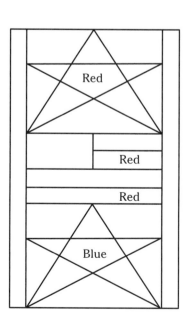

Santa Block
from America... the Pride of My Heart Quilt
photo on pages 4 - 5

The Christmas season has always been so dear to my heart. Each year as the season approaches. I am in awe of how an event that took place two thousand years ago can still affect people's lives as it does. making the world a better place in which to live. not only during the holiday season. but in some cases. for a lifetime. As I watch this magical season unfold. I feel an overwhelming desire to shout out from the rooftops. "Merry Christmas. America!"

Month 11
This Quilt Makes a Great 'Block of the Month' project

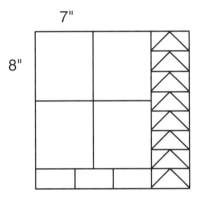

$12^1/_2$" x $14^1/_2$" (12" x 14" finished)

Santa's robe - Red Plaid
Mittens - Blue Plaid
Beard - White
Sack - Tiny Brown Check
Flag - Red Check with White Stripes
Blue with stars print
Letters - *DMC* #938 = Backstitch with 3 strands.
Tree - *DMC* #935 = Backstitch with 3 strands.
Star - *DMC* #832 = Straight stitch. Tack at each point.
Flag Pole - *DMC* Cotton Perle #5 = Color #869 - Outline stitch

If you desire to use another patriotic block instead of the Santa block, please feel free to do so. It can be anything that will fit in the 12" x 14" finished block space.

I pieced the background in this block using four different Light fabrics. If you had rather use one background piece, cut one 13" x 15" block.

After you have finished with your appliqué and embroidery, trim to $12^1/_2$" x $14^1/_2$" (12" x 14" finished). If you piece the background, cut each of four different Light fabrics 7" x 8" and join together as shown.

Square up to $12^1/_2$" x $14^1/_2$" (12" x 14" finished) when you have finished your appliqué and embroidery. Cut three $2^1/_2$" x $4^1/_2$" rectangles of different fabrics and piece to bottom of this Santa block.

Using the instructions on page 21, make eight Flying Geese rectangles and piece to the right side of your block. This makes a $16^1/_2$" square (16" finished).

Santa Block
from America... the Pride of My Heart Quilt
photo on pages 4 - 5

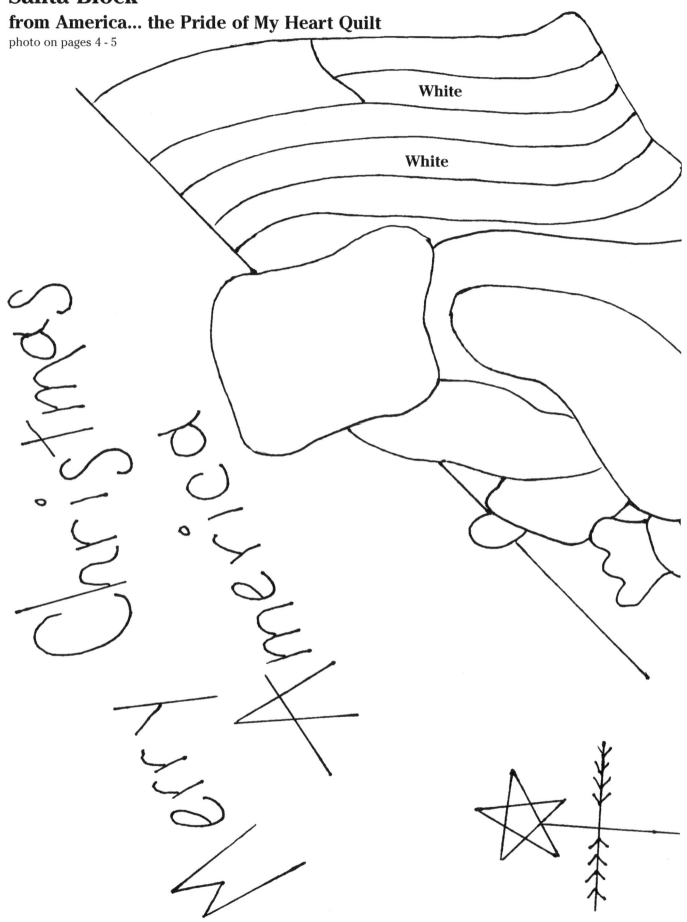

White

White

Christmas

America

Merry

Xmas

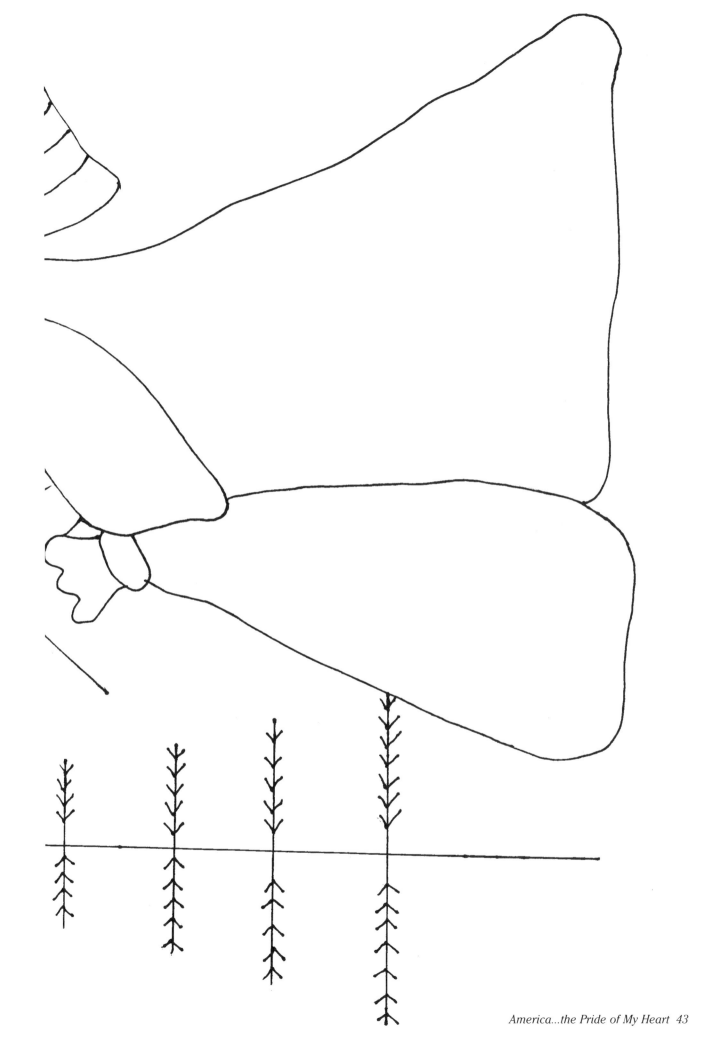

America... the Pride of My Heart Quilt
Assembly Instructions and Diagrams
photo on pages 4 - 5

Month 12
Assemble All the Blocks
This Quilt Makes a Great
'Block of the Month' project

FINISHED SIZE: 78" x 86"

Layout and Borders

1. Sawtooth Star Within Star
2. Ohio Star (8")
3. Eight-Pointed Star (16")
4. Friendship Star (8")
5. Eagle
6. Eight-Pointed Star (6")
7. Applique Star
8. Stars and Flag Block
9. Friendship Star (6")
10. Ohio Star (12")
11. Flag
12. Sawtooth Star (6")
13. Victory Basket
14. Eight-Pointed Star (8")
15. Churn Dash
16. Santa
17. Small Flag

Fill in with:
    $4^1/_2$" (4" finished) squares.
    $2^1/_2$" x $4^1/_2$" (2" x 4" finished)
        rectangles
    $2^1/_2$" s(2" finished) squares
    Four $1^1/_2$" x $6^1/_2$" (1" x 6" finished)
        strips (Navy print)

Using the layout at right, stitch the entire top together. I have marked three crosswise sections to sew together. It doesn't matter how you piece it together, but be sure to interlock all seams.

Please feel free to use a border of your choice. The borders I used are:
    First Border - (1" finished) = Navy print
        Top and bottom - $1^1/_2$" x $60^1/_2$"
        Sides - $1^1/_2$" x $70^1/_2$"
    Second Border - (6" finished) = Navy stripe
        Top and bottom $6^1/_2$" x $62^1/_2$"
        Sides - $6^1/_2$" x $70^1/_2$" plus $6^1/_2$" (6" finished)
        Sawtooth Star on each end. See pgs. 28-29.
    Third Border - (2" finished) = Scraps of Red, Blue, Gold and Brown
        Top and bottom - Cut $2^1/_2$" strips different length to measure $74^1/_2$".
        Sides - Cut $2^1/_2$" strips different lengths to measure $86^1/_2$".

Cut the borders to match your quilt rather than the sizes given above. The size of the quilt can change slightly from the pattern size because of variables in piecing or stretching.

When cutting border strips on any quilt, always measure top, bottom, and center of quilt. If there is any difference, go with the center measurement. Do the same with the sides. Always cut top and bottom borders the same length and then sew to the quilt. Do the same with the sides.

Fabric Requirements:

This is a scrap quilt. You will need several fat quarters or half yard cuts of Red, Blue, Brown, Tan and Gold fabrics.

For the borders of AMERICA... THE PRIDE OF MY HEART, you need $^1/_2$ yard of Navy fabric for the first narrow border and 1 $^1/_2$ yards of Navy Stripe for the second border.

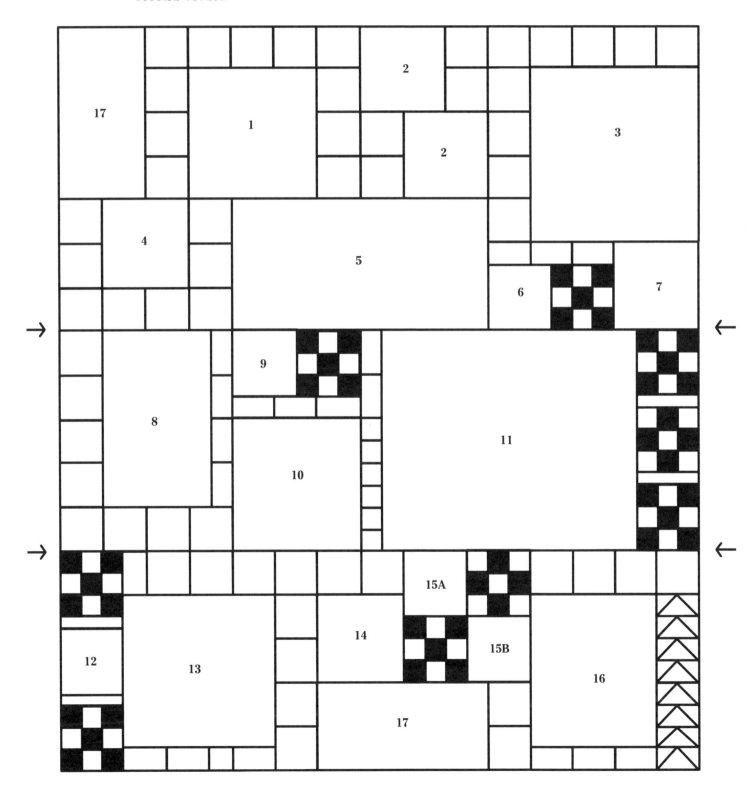

May We Never Forget
Flag Wall Hanging
photo on pages 9

May we never forget the ones who lost their lives in the terrorist attack on the World Trade Center in New York City on September 11, 2001....the day that all Americans dropped their differences and became even more united.... ready to help in any way possible....ready to fight for freedom's cause....waving the beloved Red, White, and Blue....their voices rang out, "God bless America!"

FLAG WALL HANGING
20" x 28^1/$_2$" (19^1/$_2$" x 28" finished)

Star Block - 9^1/$_2$" (9" finished)

Rotary cut
- A = One 3^1/$_2$" square (large Plaid)
- B = Four 3^1/$_2$" squares (Light Blue)
- C = Four 2" x 3^1/$_2$" rectangles (Light Blue)
- D = Four 2" x 3^1/$_2$" rectangles (Light)
- E = Four 2" squares (Light)
- F = Eight 2" squares (Blue Check)
- G = Eight 2" squares (Dark Blue Plaid)

Piece flying geese rectangles using C, D, F and G (instructions on page 21).

Line up one 2" square F on right side of rectangle D. Stitch, press and trim. Piece the other F square on opposite corner. Piece C rectangles and G squares the same way.

Using the connector square method, piece each Light 2" square E to one corner of each Light Blue 3^1/$_2$" square B.

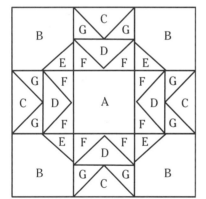

 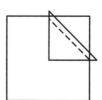

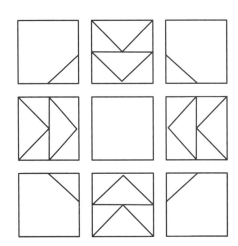

Piece entire Star block as shown at right.

Cut two $1^1/4$" x $9^1/2$" strips of Blue and piece to the top and bottom of the star block.

Cut two $1^1/4$" x 11" strips of Blue and piece to sides of the star block.

This makes an 11" ($10^1/2$" finished) block.

STRIPES

Cut 2" ($1^1/2$" finished) strips of Reds and Lights. Cut these in different lengths, none over $6^1/2$". Piece together to make sizes shown below. These Stripes are longer than the actual pattern to allow you to move them around so that the seams will off-set.

Also, when you sew several strips together, it is hard to keep the sides perfectly straight.

> Red:
> Cut four 2" x 20"
> Cut three 2" x 30"
>
> Light:
> Cut three 2" x 20"
> Cut three 2" x 30"

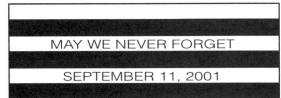

After sewing the seven short Stripes together, trim to 18" and piece to star block. Piece long Stripes together and sew to top section then trim each side to square up your flag. This flag will be approximately $19^1/2$" x 28" finished.

Transfer letters to Light Stripes and embroider with two strands of floss using the outline stitch.

I couldn't decide which color I wanted to use, *DMC* #840 or #839, so I decided to combine, using one strand of each. There is only a shade difference in the color of these two numbers, but I liked the look that I achieved by using both.

May We Never Forget
Flag Wall Hanging
photo on pages 9

GOD BLESS

MAY WE

SEPTEMBE

Align the words as needed
to fit on the stripes of your flag.

AMERICA

NEVER

FORGET

ER

11, 2001

Prairie Star Block
from "On Eagle's Wings" Quilt
photo on pages 10 - 11

The Prairie Star is a variation of the Sawtooth Star. I call it the Prairie Star because of the homespun fabrics that I used.

$10^1/_2$" (10" finished) You need eighteen of these.

Rotary cut
A = Center - Two contrasting $6^1/_2$" squares (makes 2)
B = Points - Four $3^3/_8$" squares
C = Corners - Four 3" squares
D = Geese - One $6^1/_4$" square

Place two contrasting $6^1/_2$" squares right sides together. On wrong side of Lighter fabric draw a diagonal line corner to corner.

Stitch $^1/_4$" from drawn line on both sides (Diagram A). Cut on drawn line. You now have 2 two-triangle squares. Press seam toward Darker fabric.

With right sides of contrasting triangles facing, place triangle square atop triangle square. Center diagonal seam of each interlocking seam.

Draw a diagonal line from opposite corner to corner.

Stitch $^1/_4$" from line on both sides (Diagram B). Cut on drawn line.

You now have 2 four-triangle units. Using your mini-ruler, line up diagonal line, centering on $2^3/_4$", then trim each four-triangle square to $5^1/_2$". This is your center square for your Prairie Star block.

You have an extra four-triangle square to use in another star block.

With right sides together, place 2 point squares (B) on opposite corners of "geese" square D. Draw a line diagonally from corner to corner and stitch $^1/_4$" from line on both sides (Diagram A). Cut along drawn line and press points up (Diagram B). Place remaining point squares on each "geese".

Draw a line diagonally from corner to corner and stitch $^1/_4$" from this line on both sides (Diagram C). Cut along drawn line and press points up.

You now have 4 sets of "geese" on star points.

Sew units together as shown.*

I learned this method at a retreat and I do not know the source. Since I didn't have my sewing machine. I didn't try to put one together until I got home. After many hours and repeated attempts. I finally figured the method out. My thanks to whoever is responsible for this wonderful method.

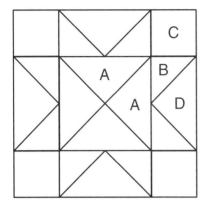

Diagram A

Diagram B

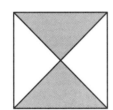

Cecil "Chick" Wilson with his dad, Hugh William Wilson on the left, and his uncle, James H. Thornton

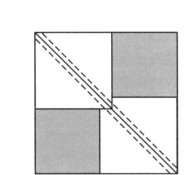

Diagram A

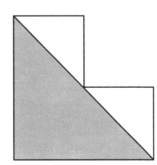

Diagram B

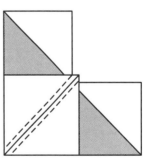

Diagram C

Alternate Blocks
from "On Eagle's Wings" Quilt

photo on pages 10 - 11

S **Louise Sheridan**
121 E. Timonium Rd.
Luthvle Timon, MD 21093

This block is called the "Snowball". It reminds me of the beauty to be found in the many states where snow decorates the landscape in the winter. Our great nation holds so many natural wonders and I appreciate the unique climates of every one.

From Alaska to Key West. America is graced with an amazing diversity that I am truly grateful to experience.

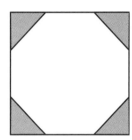

$10^1/_2$" (10" finished)
You need eighteen of these.

Cut eighteen $10^1/_2$" (10" finished) squares for alternate blocks.

Cut seventy-two 3" squares for connecting corners

Using connection corner method, piece a 3" square to each corner of the alternate blocks. Use a different fabric square in each corner for the scrappy look.

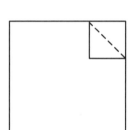

Trim and press upward. When you join the alternate blocks to star blocks, you will need to turn these seams back downward in order for the seams to interlock.

The reason I pressed them upward to begin with is because it held the shape of the alternate block better until I was ready to piece it to the star block.

My thanks to Mary Ellen Hopkins for this connecting corner method.

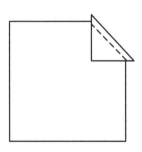

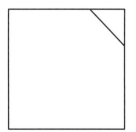

Large Appliqué Eagle
from "On Eagle's Wings" Quilt
photo on pages 10 - 11

"E PLURIBUS UNUM" is the Latin motto on the face of the Great Seal of the United States which means. "out of many. one". It refers to the creation of one nation. the United States of America. out of thirteen colonies.

Today there are fifty states standing together shoulder to shoulder in unity. America is home to someone from every nation on the planet. It is amazing that every time we have a crisis. we unite under one cause.

Our differences no longer matter. I hope that one day we will be able to unite this way without a crisis to motivate us. Our differences give us balance. Our unity makes us strong.

We as a nation must celebrate both. This eagle pattern reminds us to do so.

Cut a $16^1/_2$" x $26^1/_2$" (16" x 26" finished) background for Eagle block.

Appliqué eagle as shown using your favorite method of appliqué.

Appliqué entire wing to background, then applique body on top. I appliquéd the center piece of wing first then worked out piece by piece on each side as numbered. I appliquéd a small piece of black for the eye, but you may embroider if you desire. The tail section was appliquéd as numbered.

The wings are three different Brown Plaids and are as follows:

Fabric #1 - Sections 1-3-5-7-9-11-13

Fabric #2 - Sections 2-4-6-8-10-12

Fabric #3 - Top section of wings

When the appliqué is completed cut two $1^1/_2$" x $26^1/_2$" strips and piece to top and bottom of block. Cut two $1^1/_2$" x $18^1/_2$" strips and piece to sides.

Cut three $1^1/_2$" x $6^1/_2$" strips and two $1^1/_2$" x $5^1/_2$" strips of different fabrics. Piece together and piece to top of block. Repeat and add to bottom of block.

Cut one $1^1/_2$" x $6^1/_2$" and two $1^1/_2$" x $7^1/_2$" strips and piece to one side of block. Repeat and piece to other side. This makes a $20^1/_2$" x $30^1/_2$" (20" x 30" finished) block.

Piece entire quilt together as shown on page 61.

Large Appliqué Eagle
from "On Eagle's Wings" Quilt
photo on pages 10 - 11

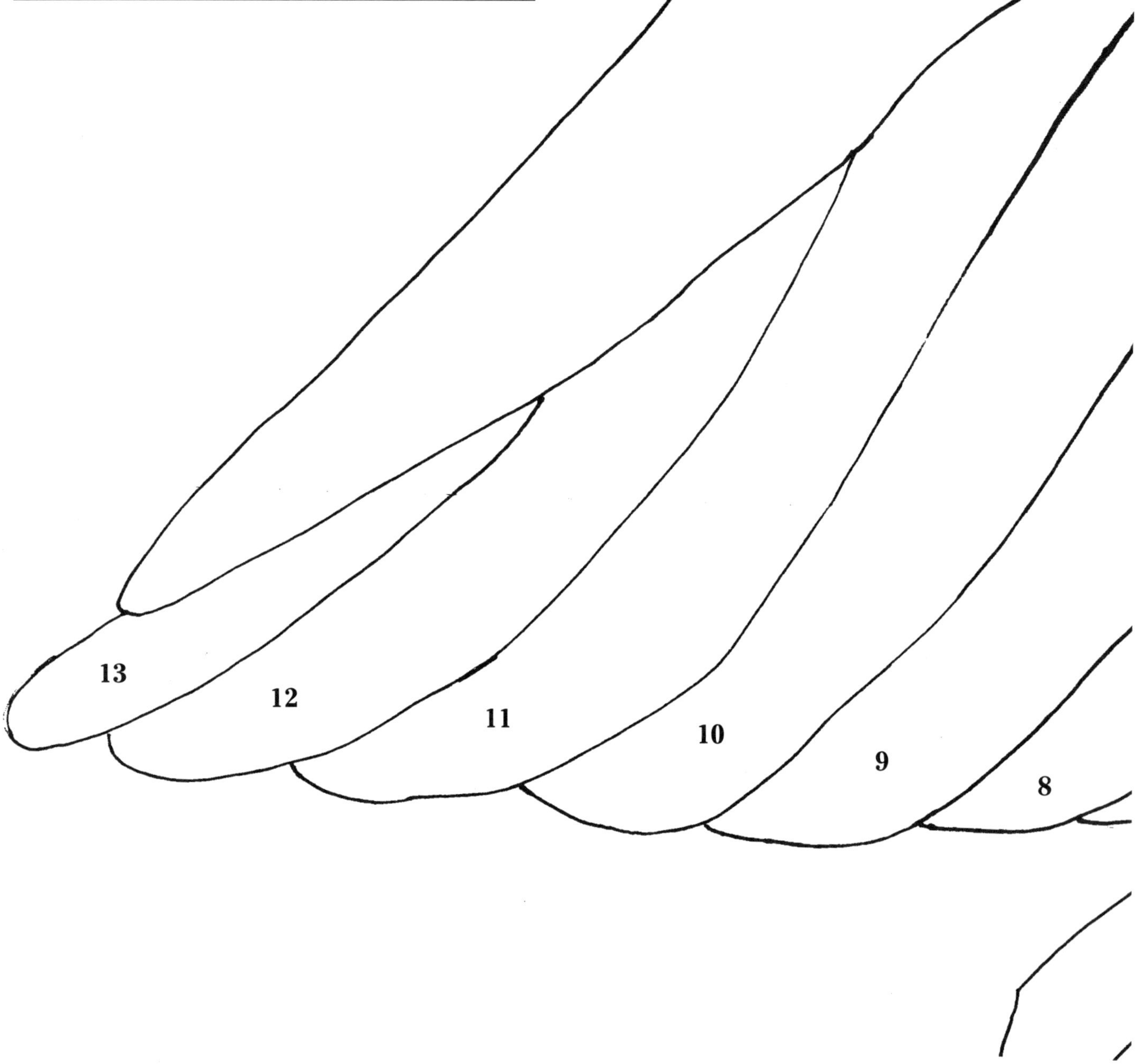

13

12

11

10

9

8

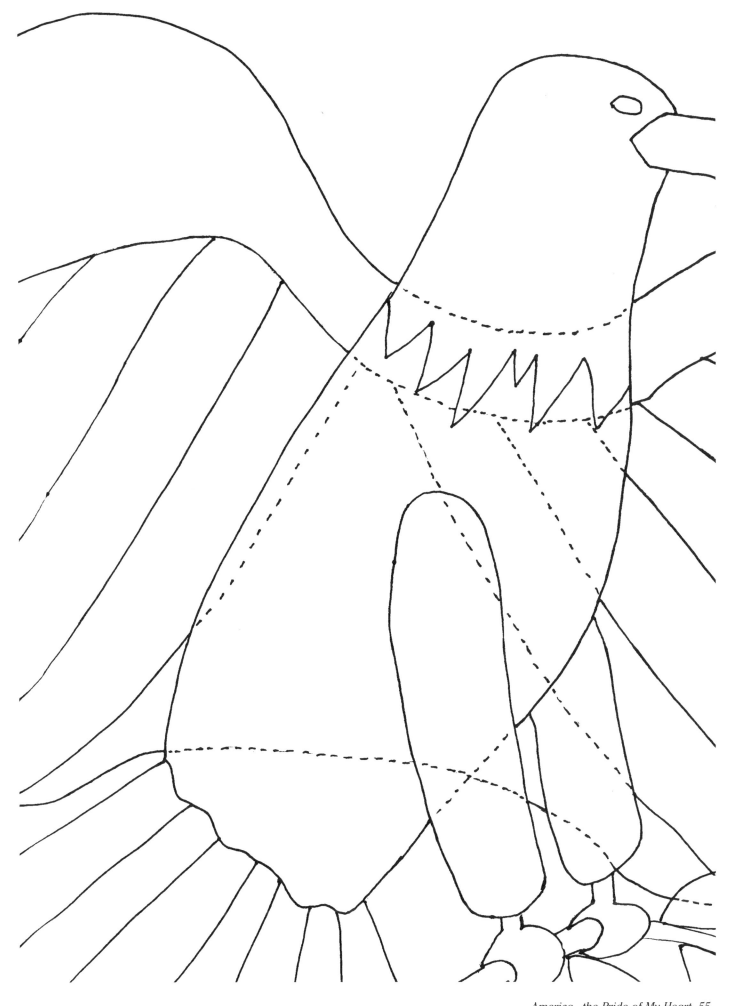

Large Appliqué Eagle
from "On Eagle's Wings" Quilt
photo on pages 10 - 11

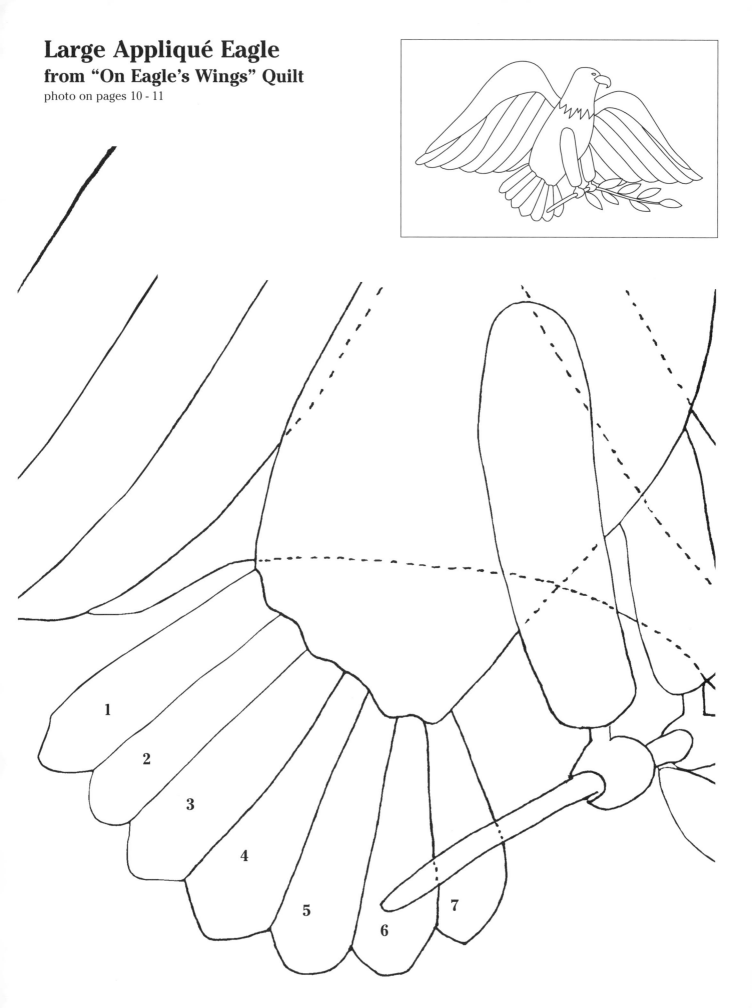

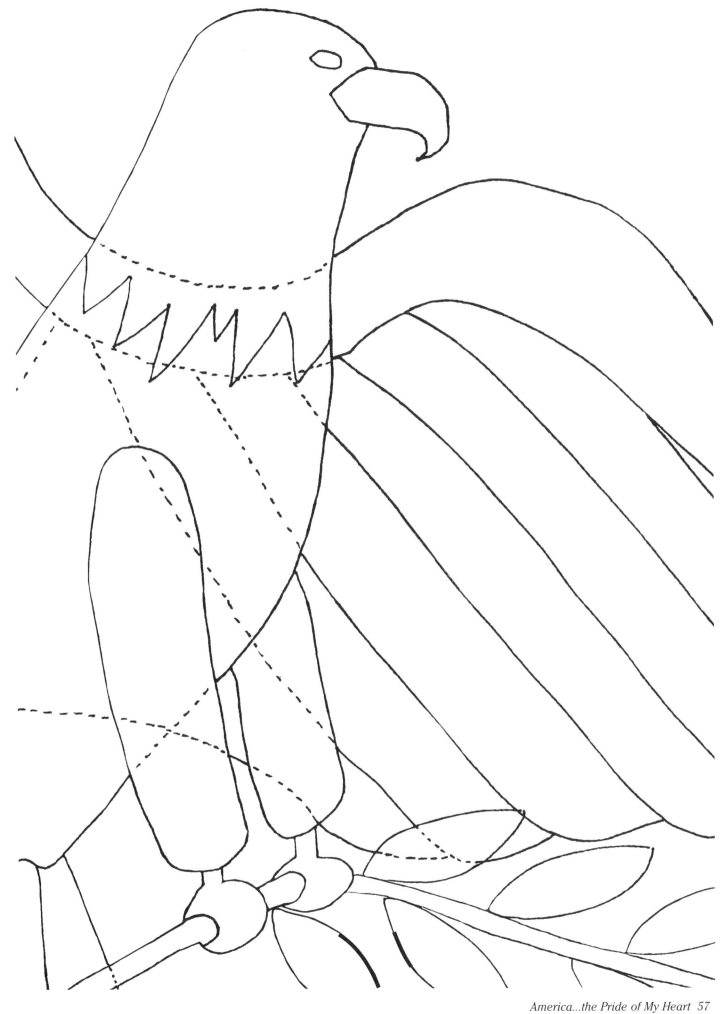

Large Appliqué Eagle
from "On Eagle's Wings" Quilt
photo on pages 10 - 11

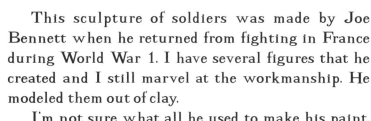

5   6   7

This sculpture of soldiers was made by Joe Bennett when he returned from fighting in France during World War 1. I have several figures that he created and I still marvel at the workmanship. He modeled them out of clay.

I'm not sure what all he used to make his paint, but I do remember that he used some face powder.

The colors are perfect. Some of these sculptures are soldiers and others are women. Most of these women are made in the image of the woman he was in love with when he went off to war.

Joe was injured in battle and didn't feel he could have a normal relationship in marriage. Therefore, he never married her, nor anyone else for that matter. The sad thing is, she never married either and both lived to be in their late 80's and lower 90's.

Of course, they were friends until they died.

'On Eagle's Wings' Quilt

Assembly Instructions and Diagrams

photo on pages 10 - 11

FINISHED SIZE: 78" x 88"

FABRIC REQUIREMENTS:

Alternate blocks and eagle back
ground = $2^1/_2$ yards

Stars, corners and second border = Assorted Plaids,
Checks, and Stripes (about 3
yards)

First border = $^2/_3$ yard

Third border and binding = $1^3/_4$
yards

First border of eagle block (Red)
= $^1/_4$ yard

Eagle Wings - Three fat quarters of contrasting Brown
Plaids

Body and legs = Brown Plaid
9" x 11"

Beak and feet = $3^1/_2$" square

Tail feathers = White 5" x 7"

Head and tail feathers =
Lighter White 5" x 8"

Vine = 4" x 10"

Leaves = 4" x 6"

Backing = $5^1/_2$ yards pieced
lengthwise

This quilt is dedicated to America's real heroes of 9/11 - the men and women of the fire departments, police, military, and citizens who risked and gave their lives to save others during the terrorist attacks in Manhattan, Washington D.C. and Pennsylvania.

May we never forget their courage and sacrifice.

BORDERS:*

First border -

Cut two $2^1/_2$" x $60^1/_2$" strips and piece to top and bottom.

Cut two $2^1/_2$" x $70^1/_2$" strips. Cut four $2^1/_2$" squares and piece a square to top and bottom of both strips.

Piece these to sides.

Second border -

Cut twenty-two $3^1/_2$" x $6^1/_2$" rectangles. Piece two strips of eleven rectangles each. Trim to $64^1/_2$" by taking in a few seams or making ends smaller. Piece to top and bottom.

Cut twenty-six $3^1/_2$" x $6^1/_2$" rectangles. Piece two strips of thirteen rectangles each. Trim to $74^1/_2$" by taking in a few seams or making ends smaller. Cut four $3^1/_2$" squares and piece a square to top and bottom of both strips.

Piece these to sides.

Third border -

Cut two $4^1/_2$" x $70^1/_2$" strips and piece these to top and bottom.

Cut two $4^1/_2$" x $80^1/_2$" strips. Cut four $4^1/_2$" squares and piece a square to top and bottom of both strips.

Piece these to sides.

*Cut the borders to match your quilt rather than the sizes given above. The size of the quilt can change slightly from the pattern size because of variables in piecing or stretching.

When cutting border strips on any quilt always measure the top, bottom, and center of the quilt. If there is any difference, go with the center measurement.

Always cut the top and bottom borders the same length and then sew to the quilt. Always cut the left and right borders the same length and then sew to the quilt.

Never sew a border strip on and cut it off at the end. Always pre-cut border strips the same length. This way your quilt will be square and not wavy.

Fabric Requirements:

This is a scrap quilt. You will need several fat quarters or half yard cuts of Red, Blue, Brown, Tan, Gold and Black fabrics.

For the borders of ON EAGLE'S WINGS, you need $^2/_3$ yard of Navy fabric for the first border, and $1\,^3/_4$ yards of Navy Stripe for the third border and binding.

Table Runner
Assembly Instructions and Diagrams
photo on pages 12 - 13

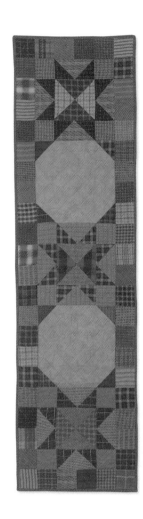

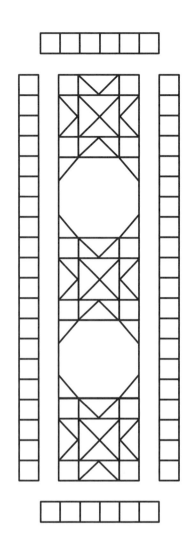

When a quilt is done. what do you do with all the little leftover scraps? Turn them into this lovely table runner in warm earth tones. Made from three pieced stars and two snow ball blocks. this project goes together very quickly.

The scrappy border will use up all those 3" squares that didn't make it into the quilt. Simple cross hatch quilting gives this runner a rustic. masculine feeling. making it very nice for your husband's den or office.

If you are decorating the dining room in the warm browns and rusts of autumn. this runner will work for you right through until Christmas.

FINISHED SIZE: 15" x 55"

Using the instructions for the Prairie Star block (pages 50-51) and the Alternate blocks (page 52) , piece three Prairie Star blocks and two alternate blocks. Piece these five blocks together as shown.

Cut fifty-two 3" squares ($2^{1}/_{2}$" finished).

Piece two strips of twenty 3" squares each and piece to the sides of runner.

Piece two strips of six 3" squares each and piece to top and bottom.

I used Hobbs 80% cotton 20% Poly batting. I utility quilted this runner using *DMC* Cotton Perlé #8.

Basic Pillow Instructions

DESIGN BLOCK:
- Make the block according to the quilt directions.
- Add side sashings. Add top and bottom sashings.
- Add side borders. Add top and bottom borders.
- Back and quilt the block as desired.
- Square up the block.

BACK OF PILLOW:
- Measure the length and width of the pillow top.
- The pillow back will be cut in 2 pieces of equal size.
- To find the width, divide the pillow top width by 2. Add 4".
- The length will be the same. Cut both back pieces.
- Turn back $1/4$" along the left edge of one piece. Fold back $1^1/2$" again along the same edge. Topstitch across the fabric through all layers close to the edge of the first fold.
- Repeat hems along the right edge of the other piece.
- Lay the pillow front flat, right side facing. Lay one back piece on top of the front so right sides face, aligning raw edges. If you used a print, make certain the motifs on both pieces are right side up.
- Lay the other back piece on the pillow top, right sides facing, aligning raw edges. Make certain the motifs on the piece are right side up.

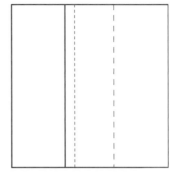

Pillow Back Diagram

The hemmed edges of the back pieces will overlap down the center of pillow.
- Pin back pieces in place on top of the pillow front, sew pillow pieces together around the raw edges.
- Turn the pillow to the right side through the back of the opening.
- Topstitch 'in the ditch' around the joining seam between the borders and the pillow center.
- Insert pillow into the back opening.

Bobby

My brother, Robert Charles (Bobby) Hanson with a group of Vietnamese children. Bobby served in the Vietnam war, fighting for the freedom that we hold so dear. Although he didn't agree with those who were protesting the war, the right for them to express their thoughts was dear to him.

Large Eagle Pillow
Applique with Wool
photo on pages 6-7

This eagle pillow makes a wonderful gift for a young person who has earned his Eagle Scout rank in the Boy Scouts of America. Presenting this gift not only expresses your pride in him. but it becomes a constant acknowledgement for accomplishing this grand achievement. as only about 4% of those who join a Boy Scout troop earn this rank.

SIZE: Fits a standard size bed pillow

Cut a 22" x 28$^1/_2$" piece of Blue Stripe for the background. Using freezer paper, cut out each pattern piece of the eagle and press it to the right side of the fabric. I used 100% wools, but any fabric will work. Position pattern pieces on the background and adhere in place with *Roxanne's* Glue-Baste-It!

Layer a piece of batting underneath your background piece and baste in place. Use your favorite applique method to attach pieces of the eagle. Using wools, I Blanket stitched around all edges of the pattern pieces.

When the applique is finished, square up the background to 21$^1/_2$" x 28". Add a piece of Red Check backing and quilt the background of the eagle. I quilted with *DMC* Cotton Perlé color #640 on every fourth Stripe, about 1$^1/_2$" apart. Serge all edges.

For the pillow back, rotary cut:
Four strips of Blue Stripe 5$^1/_2$" x 21$^1/_2$"
Four strips of Blue Check 5$^1/_2$" x 21$^1/_2$"

Using $^1/_4$" seams, piece two units of Stripe and two Check strips each, beginning with the Stripe and ending with the Check.

Layer a piece of batting and backing of Red Check underneath each unit.

Machine quilt each section. I used three horizontal rows.

Cut two strips of Blue Check 2" x 21$^1/_2$". Fold each strip and bind each section across the top of the Blue Stripe strip.

On one of the units make three buttonholes $^1/_4$" below the binding, spaced evenly apart. Serge all edges.

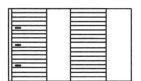

This is one of the back units of the pillow showing the button hole placement.

With right sides together, layer the unit with buttonholes (serged edges even). Layer the second unit on top of this with serged edges even. You will have a big overlap. Stitch all around using $^1/_2$" seams. Turn inside out. Sew three buttons on the bottom unit, lining up with the buttonholes.

Stuff with a standard size bed pillow. This will be a challenge, but it makes a good fit.

I am always amazed at the beauty of our great nation. No matter how many times I travel to different parts of the country. I find the "new" never wears off and the beauty takes my breath away.

One such trip is my yearly jaunt to Colorado for a quilting retreat with friends. On the drive up from Texas. the chatter is endless between the six of us. but by the time we drive the final miles through the mountains of New Mexico and Colorado. the talk always seems to die down as we are. once again. awestruck by the beauty.

For six years these dear friends and I have made this trek to spend a week in a log home on the side of a mountain. doing nothing but piecing quilts and enjoying each other and the beautiful scenery.

We share our fabrics. joys. heartaches. and lives. The best part is there is never a negative word spoken. At the end of each retreat. six beautiful quilts emerge from our pile of shared fabrics and we soak in the beauty that our hands have wrought.

This special time in my life is a reminder to me to thank God for friends. for the ability to create beauty. and for the beauty He has created which is described so well in the beloved song...

O beautiful for spacious skies.
For amber waves of grain.
For purple mountain
    majesties
Above the fruited plain!
America! America!
God shed His grace on thee
And crown thy good with
    brotherhood
From sea to shining sea.

"America the Beautiful"
by KATHERINE LEE BATES

Embroidery Stitches

Separate embroidery floss.   Use 24" lengths of floss in a #8 embroidery needle. Use 2 to 3 ply floss to outline large elements of the design and to embroider larger and more stylized patterns. Use 2 strands for the small details on some items.

Pay attention to backgrounds.   When working with lighter-colored fabrics, do not carry dark flosses across large unworked background areas. Stop and start again to prevent unsightly "ghost strings" from showing through from the front.

Blanket Stitch

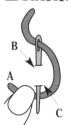

Come up at A, hold the thread down with your thumb, go down at B. Come back up at C with the needle tip over the thread. Pull the stitch into place. Repeat, outlining with the bottom legs of the stitch. Use this stitch to edge fabrics.

Running Stitch

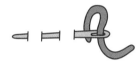

Come up at A. Weave the needle through the fabric, making short, even stitches. Use this stitch to gather fabrics, too.

Satin Stitch

Work small Straight stitches close together and at the same angle to fill an area with stitches. Vary the length of the stitches as required to keep the outline of the area smooth.

Stem Stitch or Outline Stitch

Work from left to right to make regular, slanting stitches along the stitch line. Bring the needle up above the center of the last stitch. Also called "Outline" stitch.

Straight Stitch or Stab Stitch

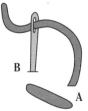

Come up at A and go down at B to form a simple flat stitch. Use this stitch for hair for animals and for simple petals on small flowers.

French Knot

Come up at A. Wrap the floss around the needle 2 - 3 times. Insert the needle close to A. Hold the floss and pull the needle through the loops gently.

Red Eagle Pillow
Applique with Wool
photo on page 67

FINISHED SIZE: 5" x 14"

Cut 2 pillow pieces of Red wool $5^{1}/_{2}$" x $14^{1}/_{2}$".

Trace pattern pieces on freezer paper.

Press the freezer paper on the right side of the following fabrics: Wings (Brown Plaid wool), Head (White wool), Beak (Gold wool).

Cut out the wool on the line because you don't have to needle-turn wool.

For the banner with the words E PLURIBUS UNUM, I used regular Tan fabric. You will need to leave seam allowance on this for the needle-turn.

Embroider the letters with 2 strands of *DMC* #898 embroidery floss using the Outline stitch.

For the shield, I used the same fabrics that I used on the larger eagle, the Blue/Stars and Red stripe. I stitched the two pieces together then needle-turned, so be sure to add seam allowance as you cut out this shield.

Cut a piece of batting and baste it to the back of the pillow top.

Position all pattern pieces in place, glue, and applique. Be sure to catch the batting or even go through it. For the wool wings, I Blanket-stitched all edges with two strands of *DMC* #869. Since the head and beak are so small, I Whip stitched the edges in place using matching thread.

Utility quilt your finished applique background piece using *DMC* Cotton Perlé color #640.

Baste a piece of batting to the back of the pillow.

With right sides together, stitch all around, leaving a small opening.

Turn and fill with Poly-fil .

Stitch the opening shut.

E PLURIBUS

UNUM